M000291068

Classic

IRISH

Classic

IRISH

A selection of the best traditional Irish food

MATTHEW DRENNAN

SMITHMARK

For Kevin, Audrey, Liam, Jimmy, Aileen, Jim, Betty and Mark with love.
This edition published in 1996
by Smithmark Publishers,
a division of U.S. Media Holdings, Inc.,
16 East 32nd Street
New York
NY 10016

SMITHMARK books are available for bulk purchase for sales promotion
and premium use. For details write or call the Manager of Special Sales,
SMITHMARK Publishers
16 East 32nd Street
New York
NY 10016
(212) 532-6600

ISBN 0 7651 9867 3

Publisher Joanna Lorenz
Senior Cookery Editor Linda Fraser
Cookery Editor Maggie Mayhew
Designer Annie Moss
Illustrator Madeleine David
Photographer Thomas Odulate
Food for photography Janet Smith, assisted by Lucy McKelvie
Stylist Marion Price
Special photography Kevin Drennan

Printed and bound in Singapore

10 9 8 7 6 5 4 3 2 1

CONTENTS

FOREWORD

As an Irishman I'm biased toward the traditional dishes and recipes of Ireland, but it's my love of everything simple and natural in the kitchen that truly draws me to this unassuming style of cooking.

In the past and perhaps in less progressive times, the national food of this country was far from "gourmet" and cooking existed to feed the appetite, not the tastebuds. However, there has been something of a renaissance in Irish cooking and today cooks all over the country are resurrecting some of the classic dishes created by this small and unassuming island.

It will become quickly apparent when cooking Irish-style, that no great culinary skills or techniques are required. This book highlights the premium products that Ireland produces – from the farmers and fishermen to the market gardeners and cheesemakers who have one common bond, their commitment to excellence.

Like the recipes themselves, the ingredients are simple and easily obtained. The key is to choose the best and the freshest – as the Irish would say, "sure, you're halfway there!"

For most of the recipes you'll find the extraordinary or exotic are few and far between; on the whole a trip to the local market will cover everything you need. Irish cooks have always been heavy handed with their use of dairy products, so I've modified some of the recipes in line with today's healthier style of living, although you'll find the odd "gallon" of cream used here and there in those recipes which would be considered too sacred to interfere with, but as they say: "a little of what you fancy does you good!"

Sláinte! (That's Irish for "cheers!")

MATTHEW DRENNAN

INTRODUCTION

If you have the pleasure of visiting any restaurant in Ireland today, you will be warmly greeted with a wealth of the world's cuisines. However, from Antrim in the north to the southernmost tip of County Kerry, you'll find, at the heart of every kitchen, a simple, honest, local approach that is classic Irish cooking.

Of course, many of Ireland's fine dishes such as Irish Stew or Colcannon were born out of necessity in poorer times, but there are two factors that have always made these simple recipes great: the land and the sea. The rich fertile soil and lush meadows nurture the finest beef, dairy products and vegetables in the world, while the miles of coastline are rich in all kinds of fish.

In a small country like Ireland, news travels fast and if a recipe is a success in one region it soon becomes a national favorite. Mysteriously though, even with something as well known as Coddle, from house to house, farm to farm or pub to pub, no two recipes are ever quite the same.

One thing that remains constant, wherever you go, is the potato. It is to the Irish people

Clonakility Blackpudding Company in County Cork (left), the rugged beauty of Brandon Creek on the Dingle Peninsula (above) and the tranquility of Lough Corrib in County Mayo (right) are but a few of the simple, natural attractions of Irish living.

what pasta is to the Italians. In fact, Ireland's bleakest period of history was in 1845–6 when the national crop failed, thus causing the great famine. Nowadays, there are no worries about that, but this versatile vegetable forms the backbone of many meals. As you will discover, it makes an appearance not just in savory dishes, but in Irish cakes and desserts, too.

Potatoes fall into two main categories: waxy and floury. For most recipes in this book the floury varieties are preferable as they mash better. Take care to peel away the minimum of skin as all the nutrients lie just beneath the surface.

They say that the only possible way to walk down any street in Ireland without passing a pub is to go into each one! So, not surprisingly, you will find that a few recipes feature one or two well-known drinks such as Guinness from Dublin, Murphy's from Cork and whiskey from just about anywhere.

Apart from soups, which are traditionally eaten with stacks of freshly baked soda bread at lunchtime, there are very few appetizers featured in this cookery book, but you could do a lot worse than enjoy a plate of fresh oysters or some thin slices of smoked salmon embellished with little more than a wedge of lemon.

Breadmaking and baking are still a very important part of Irish life, particularly in the rural areas where the day starts with soda bread and griddle cakes and ends in

the evening with a chunk of Porter Cake and a small glass of whiskey, just to help you sleep well, of course!

Irish food is simply prepared and served without fuss or ceremony. Family and good friends may come first, but good food and plenty of drink will always play host to every occasion.

LEEK AND THYME SOUP

A filling, heart-warming soup which can be blendeded to a smooth purée or served as it is here, in its original peasant style.

INGREDIENTS

2 pounds leeks
1 pound potatoes
½ cup butter
2 large thyme sprigs
1¼ cups low-fat milk
salt and ground black pepper
thyme, to garnish (optional)
4 tablespoons heavy cream,
to serve

SERVES 4

1 Trim the ends of the leeks. If you are using big winter leeks strip away all the coarser outer leaves, then cut the leeks into thick slices. Wash under cold running water.

2 Dice the potatoes coarsely into 1-inch pieces, and dry on paper towels.

3 Melt the butter in a large saucepan and add the leeks and 1 thyme sprig. Cover and cook for 4–5 minutes until softened. Add the potato pieces and just enough cold water to cover the vegetables. Re-cover and cook over low heat for 30 minutes.

4 Pour in the low-fat milk and the seasoning, cover and simmer for another 30 minutes. You will find that some of the potato breaks up, leaving you with a semi-purée and rather lumpy soup.

5 Remove the thyme sprig (the leaves will have fallen into the soup) and serve, adding a tablespoon of cream and a garnish of thyme to each portion, if using.

YELLOW BROTH

This is one of many versions of this famous Northern Irish soup which is both thickened with and given its flavor by oatmeal.

INGREDIENTS

2 tablespoons butter
1 onion, finely chopped
1 celery stalk, finely chopped
1 carrot, finely chopped
2 tablespoons flour
3¾ cups chicken stock
2 tablespoons medium oatmeal
4 ounces spinach, chopped
2 tablespoons cream
salt and ground black pepper
fresh parsley, to garnish (optional)

SERVES 4

1 Melt the butter in a large saucepan. Add the onion, celery and carrot and cook for about 2 minutes until the onion is soft.

2 Stir in the flour and cook gently for 1 minute more, stirring constantly. Pour in the chicken stock, bring to a boil and cover. Reduce the heat and simmer for 30 minutes, until the vegetables are tender.

3 Stir in the oatmeal and chopped spinach and then cook for another 15 minutes, stirring occasionally.

4 Stir in the cream and season well. Serve, garnished with parsley, if using.

CELERY SOUP

Mild celery with a hint of nutmeg – this classic creamy soup makes a perfect appetizer.

INGREDIENTS
1 small head of celery
1 onion, finely chopped
1 small garlic clove, crushed
few parsley sprigs, chopped
2 bay leaves
1 thyme sprig
2½ cups low-fat milk
2 tablespoons butter, softened
2 tablespoons flour
pinch of grated nutmeg
1 egg yolk, beaten
salt and ground black pepper
chopped fresh parsley, to garnish
croûtons, to serve

SERVES 4

COOK'S TIP
If you do not have a blender or food processor, strain the soup through a metal strainer, pressing the cooked vegetables through with the back of a spoon.

1 Break the head of celery into sticks and wash thoroughly. Trim the root ends. Chop the sticks and leaves and put them into a large saucepan.

2 Add the chopped onion, garlic, parsley, bay leaves, thyme and just enough water to cover. Bring to a boil and simmer the vegetables, uncovered, over gentle heat for about 35 minutes.

3 In a clean saucepan, bring the low-fat milk to a boil. Knead the butter and flour together to make a roux and whisk into the hot milk until just thickened. Cook over gentle heat for about 10 minutes, stirring occasionally. Pour into the celery mixture and cook for 5 minutes.

4 Remove the bay leaves and thyme. Using a ladle, spoon the soup into a blender or food processor and process for 1 minute until smooth. Return to a clean saucepan and season well.

5 Stir in the nutmeg and beaten egg yolk. Bring almost to boiling point, then serve garnished with celery leaves and croûtons.

PEA AND HAM SOUP

The main ingredient for this dish is bacon hock which is the narrow piece of bone cut from a leg of ham. You could use a piece of belly of pork instead, if you like, and remove it before serving with the finished soup.

INGREDIENTS
2½ cups green split peas
4 bacon rashers
1 onion, coarsely chopped
2 carrots, sliced
1 celery stalk, sliced
10 cups cold water
1 thyme sprig
2 bay leaves
1 large potato, coarsely diced
1 bacon hock
ground black pepper

SERVES 4

1 Put the peas into a bowl, cover with cold water and allow to soak overnight.

2 Cut the bacon into small pieces. In a large saucepan, dry-fry the bacon for 4–5 minutes or until crisp. Remove from the pan with a slotted spoon.

3 Add the chopped onion, carrots and celery stalk to the fat in the pan and cook for 3–4 minutes until the onion is softened, but not brown. Return the bacon to the pan with the water.

4 Drain the split peas and add to the pan with the thyme, bay leaves, potato and bacon hock. Bring to a boil, reduce the heat, cover and cook gently for 1 hour.

5 Remove the thyme, bay leaves and hock. Process the soup in a blender or food processor until smooth. Return to a clean pan. Cut the meat from the hock and add to the soup. Season with lots of black pepper.

NETTLE SOUP

A country-style soup which is a tasty variation of the classic Irish potato soup. Use wild nettles if you can find them, or a washed head of round lettuce if you prefer.

INGREDIENTS
½ cup butter
1 pound large onions, sliced
1 pound potatoes, cut into chunks
3 cups chicken stock
1 ounce nettle leaves
small bunch of chives, snipped
salt and ground black pepper
heavy cream, to serve

SERVES 4

1 Melt the butter in a large saucepan and add the sliced onions. Cover and cook for 5 minutes until just softened. Add the potatoes to the saucepan with the chicken stock. Cover and cook for 25 minutes.

2 Wearing rubber gloves, remove the nettle leaves from their stalks. Wash the leaves under cold running water, then dry on paper towels. Add to the saucepan and cook for another 5 minutes.

3 Ladle the soup into a blender or food processor and process until smooth. Return to a clean saucepan and season well. Stir in the chives and serve with a swirl of cream and a dash of pepper.

ROAST CHICKEN WITH HERB AND ORANGE BREAD STUFFING

Tender roast chicken scented with orange and herbs, served with a light gravy.

INGREDIENTS

2 onions
2 tablespoons butter
2½ cups soft white bread crumbs
2 tablespoons chopped fresh mixed herbs
grated rind of 1 orange
3½-pound chicken with giblets
1 carrot, sliced
1 bay leaf
1 thyme sprig
3¾ cups cold water
1 tablespoon tomato paste
2 teaspoons cornstarch, mixed with
1 tablespoon cold water
salt and ground black pepper
chopped fresh parsley, to garnish

SERVES 4–6

1 Preheat the oven to 400°F. Finely chop 1 onion. Melt the butter in a pan and add the onion. Cook for 3–4 minutes until soft. Stir in the bread crumbs, fresh herbs and orange rind. Season well.

2 Remove the giblets from the chicken and put aside. Wash the cavity of the chicken and dry well with paper towels. Spoon in the herb and orange stuffing, then rub a little butter into the breast and season it well. Put the chicken into a roasting pan and cook in the oven for 20 minutes, then reduce the heat to 350°F and cook for another hour.

3 Put the giblets, the other onion, the carrot, bay leaf, thyme and cold water into a large pan. Bring to a boil, then simmer while the chicken is roasting.

4 Remove the chicken from the pan. Skim off the fat from the pan juices, strain the juices and stock into a pan and discard the giblets and vegetables. Simmer for about 5 more minutes. Whisk in the tomato paste.

5 Whisk the cornstarch paste into the gravy and cook for 1 minute. Season well and serve with the chicken, garnished with parsley.

CHICKEN, LEEK AND BACON CASSEROLE

 moist whole chicken, braised on a bed of leeks and bacon and topped with a creamy tarragon sauce.

INGREDIENTS

1 tablespoon vegetable oil
2 tablespoons butter
3½-pound chicken
8 ounces streaky bacon
1 pound leeks
1 cup chicken stock
1 cup heavy cream
1 tablespoon chopped fresh tarragon
salt and ground black pepper

SERVES 4–6

1 Preheat the oven to 350°F. Heat the oil and melt the butter in a large flameproof casserole. Add the chicken and cook it breast side down for 5 minutes until golden. Remove from the casserole.

2 Dice the bacon and add to the casserole. Cook for 4–5 minutes until golden.

3 Trim the leeks, cut them into 1-inch pieces and add to the bacon. Cook for 5 minutes until the leeks begin to brown. Put the chicken on top of the bacon and leeks. Cover and put into the oven. Cook for 1½ hours.

4 Remove the chicken, bacon and leeks from the casserole. Skim the fat from the juices. Pour in the stock and the cream and bring to a boil. Cook for 4–5 minutes until slightly reduced and thickened.

5 Stir in the tarragon and seasoning (it may only need pepper). Serve chicken slices with the bacon, leeks and a little sauce.

CODDLE

S troll around Dublin on a Saturday night and you will find numerous variations of this traditional favorite dish. The basic ingredients, however, are the same wherever you go – potatoes, sausages and bacon.

INGREDIENTS
4 bacon rashers
1 tablespoon vegetable oil
2 large onions, chopped
2 garlic cloves, crushed
8 large pork sausages
4 large potatoes
¼ teaspoon dried sage
1¼ cups chicken stock
2 tablespoons chopped fresh parsley
salt and ground black pepper
soda bread, to serve

SERVES 4

1 Preheat the oven to 350°F. Cut the bacon into 1-inch strips.

2 Heat the oil in a frying pan and fry the bacon for 2 minutes. Add the onions and cook for another 5–6 minutes until golden. Add the garlic and cook for 1 minute, then remove from the pan and set aside.

3 Add the pork sausages to the frying pan and cook on all sides for 5–6 minutes until golden brown.

4 Slice the potatoes thinly and arrange in the base of a large, buttered ovenproof dish. Spoon the bacon and onion mixture on top. Season with the ground black pepper and sprinkle with the sage.

5 Pour on the chicken stock and top with the sausages. Cover and cook in the oven for 1 hour. Serve with fresh soda bread.

BOILED HAM AND CABBAGE

 no-nonsense dish that is full of warming winter flavors and very easy to make.

INGREDIENTS
2½ pounds ham, in one piece
2 bay leaves
12 peppercorns
1 celery stalk
1–2 onions, halved
2 large carrots
1 large Savoy cabbage
salt and ground black pepper
chopped fresh parsley, to garnish
boiled potatoes, to serve (optional)

SERVES 6

1 Drain the water from the ham if you have soaked it. Weigh the meat to calculate the cooking time. Put the ham into a large saucepan and cover with cold water.

2 Add the bay leaves, peppercorns, celery stalk, onions and carrots. Bring to a boil, reduce the heat, cover and simmer for 25 minutes per pound plus 25 minutes.

3 Carefully lift out the ham and set it aside. Drain the cooking liquid into a clean saucepan and bring to a boil.

4 Meanwhile, discard the outer leaves of the cabbage. Tear the remaining leaves, including the heart, into pieces, discarding any of the tough stalks. Add to the cooking liquid and cook, uncovered, for 20 minutes until tender. Taste for seasoning – you may not have to add any.

5 Serve slices of the warm ham on a bed of cabbage with a little of the cooking liquid poured over the top. Garnish with the chopped parsley and serve with boiled potatoes, if liked.

COOK'S TIP
It is always difficult to tell how salty a piece of ham is going to be unless you buy it from a regular source. If in doubt, soak it in cold water for several hours or overnight, changing the water at least once.

RABBIT STEW

This is a hearty winter stew which includes the classic combination of rabbit and lima beans, delicately flavored with garlic and bacon.

INGREDIENTS
¾ cup lima beans
3 pounds rabbit, cut into pieces
2 tablespoons flour
2 tablespoons lard
2 bacon rashers, finely chopped
1 onion, chopped
1 garlic clove, crushed
1 tablespoon tomato paste
1 pound carrots, sliced
1 celery stalk, sliced
2 bay leaves
2½ cups chicken stock
salt and ground black pepper
mashed potato, to serve (optional)

SERVES 4

1 Put the butter beans into a bowl, cover with cold water and let soak thoroughly overnight.

2 Preheat the oven to 350°F. Put the rabbit pieces, flour and seasoning into a bag and shake until the rabbit pieces are well and evenly coated.

3 Melt the lard in a flameproof casserole. Fry the rabbit over medium heat until golden. Remove from the dish and set aside. Add the bacon, onion and garlic and cook for 4–5 minutes until the onion is just soft.

4 Stir in the tomato paste and cook for 1 minute. Return the rabbit to the dish with the carrot, celery and bay leaves. Pour in the stock, cover and cook for 1 hour.

5 Remove from the oven. Drain the lima beans and stir them into the casserole. Replace the lid and return to the oven for another 50 minutes. Check the seasoning and serve with mashed potato, if liked.

IRISH STEW

Simple and delicious, this is the quintessential Irish main course. Traditionally, mutton chops are used, but as they are harder to find these days you can use lamb instead.

INGREDIENTS

2½ pounds boneless lamb chops
1 tablespoon vegetable oil
3 large onions
4 large carrots
3¾ cups water
4 large potatoes, cut into chunks
1 large thyme sprig
1 tablespoon butter
1 tablespoon chopped fresh parsley
salt and ground black pepper
Savoy cabbage, to serve (optional)

SERVES 4

1 Trim any fat from the lamb. Heat the oil in a flameproof casserole and brown the meat on both sides. Remove from the pan.

2 Cut the onions into quarters and thickly slice the carrots. Add to the casserole and cook for 5 minutes until the onions are browned. Return the meat to the pan with the water. Bring to a boil, reduce the heat, cover and simmer for 1 hour.

3 Add the potatoes to the pan with the thyme and cook for another hour.

4 Leave the stew to settle for a few minutes. Remove the fat from the liquid with a ladle, then pour off the liquid into a clean saucepan. Stir in the butter and the parsley. Season well and pour back into the casserole. Serve with Savoy cabbage, if liked.

SPICED BEEF

Christmas in Ireland would not be complete without a cold side of spiced beef to see you through the holiday season. Make sure you allow plenty of time (at least ten days) for the meat to absorb the spices and marinade, as this is what makes it so tender and full of flavor.

INGREDIENTS

1 cup sea salt
2½ pounds silverside of beef or brisket, boned and untied
4 tablespoons brown sugar
½ teaspoon ground allspice
½ teaspoon ground cloves
½ teaspoon grated nutmeg
1 bay leaf, crushed
1 tablespoon saltpeter
1 tablespoon molasses
2 carrots, sliced
1 onion, quartered
ground black pepper
pickles and bread, to serve (optional)

SERVES 8

1 Rub the salt into the beef and leave in a cool place overnight.

2 In a bowl, mix the brown sugar, allspice, cloves, nutmeg, bay leaf, saltpeter and ground black pepper. Remove the beef from the salt and juices and wipe dry with paper towels. Sprinkle with the spice mixture and leave in a cool place overnight.

3 Lightly warm the molasses and pour it on the meat. Allow to marinate for 1 week, turning once a day.

4 Roll up the beef and secure it with string. Put it into a large pan of boiling water with the carrots and onion. Bring to a boil, lower the heat, cover and simmer for 3 hours. Let cool in the liquid.

5 Transfer the beef to a board or a large plate. Balance another board on top, weight it down and leave for at least 8 hours. Carve and serve the meat cold with pickles and bread, if desired.

STEAK WITH STOUT AND POTATOES

This recipe uses the finest and most famous of all the Emerald Isle's ingredients: Irish beef, Murphy's stout from Cork and, of course, potatoes. You can use any stout, but Murphy's is less bitter than most.

INGREDIENTS
1½ pounds stewing beef
1 tablespoon vegetable oil
2 tablespoons butter
8 ounces baby white onions
¾ cup stout or dark beer
1¼ cups beef stock
bouquet garni
1½ pounds potatoes, cut into thick slices
8 ounces large mushrooms, sliced
1 tablespoon flour
½ teaspoon mild mustard
salt and ground black pepper
chopped thyme sprigs, to garnish

SERVES 4

1 Trim any excess fat from the steak and cut into four pieces. Season both sides of the meat. Heat the oil and half the butter in a large heavy pan. Brown the meat on both sides, taking care not to burn the butter. Remove from the pan and set aside.

2 Add the baby white onions to the pan and brown for 3–4 minutes. Return the steak to the pan. Pour on the stout or beer and stock and season to taste.

3 Add the bouquet garni and top with the potato slices. Cover with a tight-fitting lid and simmer over gentle heat for 1 hour.

4 Add the sliced mushrooms. Replace the lid and cook for another 30 minutes. Remove the meat and vegetables with a slotted spoon and arrange on a platter.

5 Mix the remaining butter with the flour to make a roux. Whisk a little at a time into the cooking liquid. Stir in the mustard. Cook for 2–3 minutes until thickened. Season and pour on the meat. Garnish with plenty of thyme sprigs.

COOK'S TIP
Put the onions in a bowl and cover with boiling water. Let soak for about 5 minutes and drain. The skins should peel away easily.

GUINNESS AND OYSTER PIE

 ayers of crisp puff pastry encase a tasty rich stew of tender beef and fresh oysters.

INGREDIENTS
1 pound stewing beef
2 tablespoons flour
1 tablespoon vegetable oil
2 tablespoons butter
1 onion, sliced
⅔ cup Guinness
⅔ cup beef stock
1 teaspoon sugar
bouquet garni
12 oysters, opened
12 ounces puff pastry
1 egg, beaten
salt and ground black pepper
chopped fresh parsley, to garnish

SERVES 4

1 Preheat the oven to 350°F. Trim any excess fat from the meat and cut into 1-inch pieces. Place in a bag with the flour and plenty of seasoning. Shake until the meat is well coated.

2 Heat the oil and butter in a flameproof casserole and fry the meat for 10 minutes until well sealed and browned all over. Add the onion and continue cooking for 2–3 minutes until just softened.

3 Pour in the Guinness and stock. Add the sugar and bouquet garni. Cover and cook in the oven for 1¼ hours.

4 Remove from the oven, spoon into a 5-cup pie pan and set aside to cool for 15 minutes. Increase the oven temperature to 400°F.

5 Meanwhile, remove the oysters from their shells and wash. Dry on paper towels and stir into the beef and Guinness.

6 Roll out the pastry large enough to fit the pie pan. Brush the edge of the pan with the beaten egg and lay the pastry over the top. Trim neatly and decorate. Brush with the remaining egg and cook for 25 minutes until puffed and golden. Serve at once garnished with parsley.

SHRIMP WITH GARLIC BREAD CRUMBS

Fresh Dublin Bay shrimp, also known by their French name, *langoustine*, are a delight to eat, especially when smothered in garlic butter and topped with fresh golden bread crumbs. Halve this recipe for appetizer portions.

INGREDIENTS
32 jumbo shrimp
1½ cups butter, softened
8 garlic cloves, chopped
2 tablespoons chopped fresh parsley
4 scallions, finely chopped
1 tablespoon whole-grain mustard
2 cups fresh white bread crumbs
ground black pepper
fresh parsley, to garnish
brown bread, to serve

SERVES 4

1 Bring a large pan of water to a boil. Drop in the shrimp. Cook until they float on top of the water. Drain and refresh under cold water, then shell.

2 Preheat the oven to 400°F. Place the butter, garlic, parsley, scallions, mustard and plenty of ground black pepper in a bowl. Beat until well blended.

3 Divide the shrimp among four individual ovenproof dishes. Divide the butter among them and spread it over the shrimp with the back of a knife. Sprinkle with the fresh bread crumbs.

4 Place the dishes in the oven and cook for about 15 minutes, or until the bread-crumbs are golden brown. Garnish the dishes with fresh parsley and serve with brown bread.

DRESSED CRAB

D ressed crab has topped the menu in Irish restaurants for many years. It is traditionally served in the crab shell, but you could use individual ovenproof dishes if you prefer.

INGREDIENTS

⅔ cup milk

3 tablespoons butter

1 tablespoon plain flour

12 ounces fresh white crabmeat

1 teaspoon French mustard

5 cups fresh bread crumbs

2 tablespoons snipped fresh chives

salt and ground black pepper

snipped chives and chopped parsley,

to garnish

SERVES 4

1 Preheat the oven to 400°F. Bring the milk to a boil. In another saucepan, melt 1 tablespoon of the butter. Stir in the flour and cook for 1 minute. Gradually whisk in the milk, a little at a time, until smooth and thick. Cook over gentle heat for 5 minutes. Allow to cool.

2 Put the crabmeat into a bowl with the mustard, 2½ cups of the bread crumbs and the snipped chives. Season with salt and ground black pepper. Stir into the white sauce and mix well.

3 Spoon the mixture into the crab shells or into dishes. Sprinkle with the remaining bread crumbs and dot with the remaining butter. Bake for 20 minutes. Garnish with the parsley and chives and serve.

SOLE IN A GREEN JACKET

resh fillets of sole, wrapped in lettuce, gently poached and served with the lightest white wine sauce.

INGREDIENTS
4 fresh sole fillets, about 6 ounces each
1 large head of Boston lettuce
2 shallots, finely chopped
1 bay leaf
1¼ cups dry white wine
1¼ cups sweet butter, softened
1 tablespoon snipped fresh chives
salt and ground black pepper
boiled potatoes, to serve (optional)

SERVES 4

1 Preheat the oven to 350°F. Using a very sharp knife, skin the sole fillets. Insert the blade of the knife between the skin and the fillet at the tail end, then, holding the skin with one hand, glide the knife along the skin to remove the fillet.

2 Bring a large saucepan of water to a boil. Separate the lettuce leaves and drop them into the water for 1 minute. Remove with a slotted spoon and refresh under cold water. Drain well.

3 Lay out 3–4 leaves and put a sole fillet on top. Season well and wrap the leaves around the fish. Top with more leaves, if necessary. Put the fish into a large buttered dish and pour in a little water. Cover with buttered paper and cook for 15 minutes.

4 Meanwhile, put the shallots, bay leaf and white wine into a saucepan. Cook over high heat for 5 minutes until reduced to about 4–5 tablespoons.

5 Remove the bay leaf. Whisk in the butter a little at a time until the sauce is smooth and glossy. Strain into a clean pan. Stir in the chives and season well. Do not boil. Lift the wrapped fish out of the dish and serve with the sauce and boiled potatoes, if liked.

SEAFOOD PIE

There are as many variations of this dish as there are fish in the sea. You can change the fish and shellfish in this recipe according to what is fresh and available.

INGREDIENTS

1 pound fish bones, cleaned
6 peppercorns
1 small onion, sliced
1 bay leaf
3 cups cold water
2 pounds smoked haddock
8 ounces raw shrimp
1 pound mussels, cleaned
1½ pounds potatoes
5 tablespoons butter
2 tablespoons flour
12 ounces leeks, sliced
4 ounces small button mushrooms, sliced
1 tablespoon chopped fresh tarragon
1 tablespoon chopped fresh parsley
salt and ground black pepper
fresh tarragon, to garnish

SERVES 4

1 Put the fish bones, peppercorns, onion and bay leaf into a small saucepan with the cold water. Bring to a boil, reduce the heat and simmer for 20 minutes. Remove from the heat and set aside.

2 Meanwhile, put the smoked haddock into a pan with just enough water to cover it. Cover with a piece of buttered paper and simmer for 15 minutes. Drain and cool, then remove the bones and skin and put the flaked fish into a bowl.

3 Drop the shrimp into a pan of boiling water and cook until they begin to float. Drain and refresh under cold running water. Peel and discard the shells and add the shrimp to the bowl of flaked fish.

4 Place the mussels in a saucepan with 2 tablespoons of water. Cover and cook over high heat for 5–6 minutes until the mussels have opened. Discard any that have not. Refresh under cold water and remove the shells. Put the cooked mussels into the bowl with the fish and shrimp.

5 Boil the potatoes for 20 minutes. Drain and dry over high heat for 1 minute until all traces of moisture have evaporated. Mash with 2 tablespoons of the butter.

6 Meanwhile, melt 2 tablespoons of the butter in a saucepan. Stir in the flour and cook for 1 minute. Strain the fish stock and measure 2½ cups. Whisk a little at a time into the roux until smooth. Cook over gentle heat for 10 minutes.

7 Preheat the oven to 350°F. Melt the remaining butter in another saucepan, add the leeks and mushrooms and cook for 4–5 minutes, taking care not to brown them. Add to the fish. Stir in the chopped herbs. Pour in the sauce and fold together, then spoon into a baking dish. Spoon on the mashed potatoes and smooth level with a fork. Place in the oven and cook for 30 minutes. Garnish with the tarragon.

COD WITH PARSLEY SAUCE

Many moons ago, when cod was more plentiful and cheaper than it is today, this was a commonplace, yet undervalued, dish. Perhaps it is time to rediscover just what a delicious recipe it is.

INGREDIENTS
4 cod fillets or steaks, about 8 ounces each
1 bay leaf
6 peppercorns
small bunch of parsley
1 shallot, quartered
2 tablespoons butter
2 tablespoons flour
1¼ cups low fat milk
salt and ground black pepper
cabbage, to serve (optional)

SERVES 4

1 Grease a large flameproof casserole with a little butter. Lay the four cod fillets in the pan, skin side down. Add the bay leaf, peppercorns, parsley stalks and the shallot.

2 Pour on enough cold water to cover the fish. Slowly bring to a boil and reduce quickly to a gentle simmer. Cook for 5 minutes. Meanwhile, finely chop the parsley tops and set aside.

3 Melt the butter in a saucepan, then stir in the flour and cook gently for 1 minute. Strain the stock from the fish and reserve ⅔ cup. Remove the fish from the pan and keep warm. Gradually add the reserved stock to the flour mixture and continue stirring over medium heat until smooth and thickened.

4 Gradually add the milk and bring to a boil. Reduce the heat and cook for about 10 minutes, stirring occasionally. Stir in the chopped parsley and season well. Serve the sauce with the fish and cabbage, if desired.

SALMON
WITH SORREL

A luxurious, yet surprisingly light, combination of delicate flavors makes this the perfect recipe for entertaining Irish style.

INGREDIENTS
8 ounces fish bones
1 small onion, sliced
3–4 peppercorns
1 bay leaf
few parsley stalks
1¼ cups cold water
2 tablespoons butter, melted
4 salmon fillets, about 6 ounces each
½ cup dry white wine
1¼ cups light cream
3 ounces sorrel, washed
salt and ground black pepper

SERVES 4

1 Preheat the oven to 400°F. Wash the fish bones and put into a saucepan with the onion, peppercorns, bay leaf and parsley stalks. Add the cold water. Bring to a boil, reduce the heat and simmer for 20 minutes.

2 Brush an ovenproof dish with some of the melted butter. Lay the salmon fillets on top and brush with the remaining butter. Bake for 10 minutes, until just cooked.

3 Meanwhile, strain ⅔ cup of the stock into a saucepan. Add the white wine and cook over high heat until the liquid is reduced by half.

COOK'S TIP
Sorrel is a herb which grows wild in the countryside and has a refreshing, slightly sour taste reminiscent of lemons. Most readily available in the summer, it is often used in soups and sauces. Make the most of its flavor by adding it at the end of the recipe.

4 Pour in the cream and bring to a boil. Reduce the heat and simmer until the sauce just coats a spoon, then season. Tear the sorrel into pieces and add to the sauce. Cook for 1 minute. Serve with the salmon.

WRAPPED SALMON AND RICE

A close cousin of the Russian Koulibiaca, this Irish dish is made with chunks of fresh salmon, combined with mushrooms, eggs and rice in light and flaky pastry.

INGREDIENTS
1 pound skinned and boned
fresh salmon fillet
4 ounces button mushrooms
6 scallions
4 tablespoons butter
2 eggs, hard-boiled
1 cup long-grain rice, cooked
juice of ½ lemon
1 pound puff pastry
1 egg, beaten
salt and ground black pepper
hollandaise sauce, to serve

SERVES 4

1 Preheat the oven to 400°F. Put the salmon into a saucepan with just enough water to cover it. Poach it gently for 10 minutes until just cooked. Drain and then let cool.

2 Roughly chop the mushrooms and finely slice the scallions. Melt the butter in a saucepan and cook the mushrooms and scallions for 2–3 minutes. Place them in a mixing bowl.

3 Flake the fish and add to the mushroom and scallion mixture. Shell the hard-boiled eggs, then chop and stir into the salmon mixture with the rice. Stir in the lemon juice and season well with salt and pepper.

4 Roll out the puff pastry to a rectangle 12 x 14 inches. Brush the edges with egg. Spoon the filling into the center of the pastry. Join the edges and seal the sides and ends with egg.

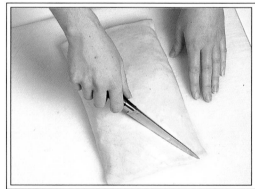

5 Score the top of the pastry with a knife and brush with the remaining egg. Bake for about 30 minutes until golden. Serve hot with hollandaise sauce, or let cool completely and serve cold.

COLCANNON

 famous and delicious southern Irish dish which is traditionally served with broiled sausages and bacon.

INGREDIENTS

2 pounds potatoes

1 Savoy cabbage

4 tablespoons butter

1 small onion, finely chopped

1 tablespoon chopped fresh parsley

salt and ground black pepper

SERVES 4

1 Cut the potatoes into equal chunks. Place in a saucepan and cover with cold water. Bring to a boil, reduce the heat, cover and simmer for 20 minutes.

2 Drain the potatoes and dry out over high heat for 1 minute until all traces of moisture have evaporated, then mash them.

3 Meanwhile, bring another pan of water to a boil. Break off the outer cabbage leaves and discard. Tear the remaining leaves into pieces and cook in the boiling water for 15 minutes, until just tender.

4 Melt the butter in a large frying pan and heat until hot. Add the chopped onion and cook for 3–4 minutes until just soft.

5 Add the mashed potato and cabbage and fry for 5 minutes, stirring occasionally until it begins to brown around the edges. Stir in the chopped parsley and season well. Serve with broiled sausages and bacon.

GRIDDLE CAKES

T hese are sometimes called potato cakes or scones, but whatever you call them they are delicious served hot with butter and jam, or with bacon for a hearty breakfast.

INGREDIENTS

8 ounces potatoes
1 cup flour
¼ teaspoon salt
¼ teaspoon baking powder
1 tablespoon butter
1½ tablespoons milk

MAKES 6

1 Cut the potatoes into equal chunks. Place in a saucepan and cover with cold water. Bring to a boil, reduce the heat and simmer for 20 minutes until tender.

2 Drain the potatoes and dry out over a high heat for 1 minute, until all traces of moisture have evaporated. Mash well, making sure there are no lumps left.

3 Sift the flour, salt and baking powder into a mixing bowl. Rub in the butter with your fingertips.

4 Add the mashed potato and mix thoroughly with a fork. Make a well in the center and pour in the milk. Bring the mixture together to form a smooth dough.

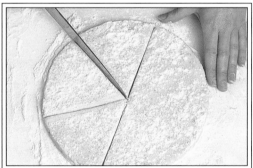

5 Turn out onto a floured board and knead. Roll out to a round ¼-inch thick. Cut in half, then cut each half into three triangles.

6 Grease a griddle or frying pan with some butter and heat until very hot. Fry the cakes for 3–4 minutes until golden brown, turning once, then serve hot.

RUTABAGA AND POTATO STUFFING

An unusual and delicious alternative to bread and bulk sausage stuffings. This amount is enough to fill a 6-pound turkey.

INGREDIENTS
2 pounds potatoes
1 large rutabaga
8 tablespoons butter
4 bacon rashers, finely chopped
1 large onion, finely chopped
1 large thyme sprig
salt and ground black pepper

SERVES 8

1 Cut the potatoes into equal-size pieces. Place in a saucepan and cover with cold water. Bring to a boil, reduce the heat and cover. Cook for 20 minutes.

2 Meanwhile, cut the rutabaga into chunks. Place in a saucepan and cover with cold water. Bring to a boil, reduce the heat and cook for 20 minutes.

3 Drain both the potatoes and rutabaga and dry out over a high heat for 1 minute, until all traces of moisture have evaporated. Transfer them both to a bowl.

4 Melt the butter in a pan and fry the bacon for 3–4 minutes. Add the chopped onion and fry for another 3–4 minutes until soft. Sprinkle on the thyme leaves.

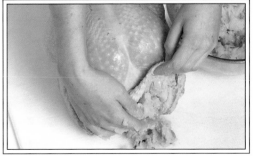

5 Stir into the vegetables. Season well and mash until smooth. Use to stuff turkey and roasts as usual, or put into an ovenproof dish and cover with foil. Bake in the oven for the final hour of the meat's cooking time.

CHAMP

Simple but undeniably tasty, Champ makes an excellent companion for a hearty stew. Use a floury potato for a better result.

INGREDIENTS
2 pounds potatoes
1 small bunch scallions
⅔ cup milk
4 tablespoons butter
salt and ground black pepper

SERVES 4

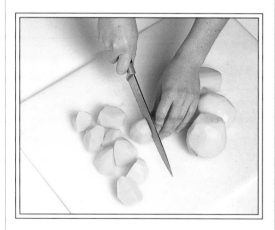

1 Cut the potatoes into even-size chunks, place in a pan and cover with cold water. Bring to a boil, reduce the heat, cover and simmer for 20 minutes until tender.

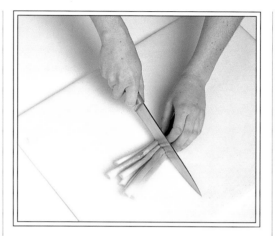

2 Cut the green stems from the scallions and set aside. Finely chop the remaining scallions and put them into a saucepan with the milk. Bring to a boil and simmer until just soft.

3 Drain the potatoes well and put them back into the saucepan. Return to the heat for 1 minute until all traces of moisture have evaporated.

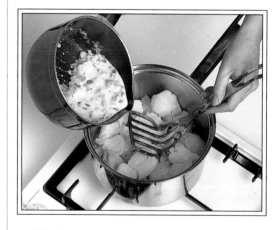

4 Mash the potatoes with the milk and scallions and season well. Serve with the butter melting on top and garnish with the chopped green stems of the scallions.

CHOCOLATE CARRAGHEEN
WITH IRISH COFFEE SAUCE

An impressive-looking dessert that is extremely simple to make. The secret ingredient is sure to keep dinner-party guests guessing.

INGREDIENTS
2½ cups milk
¾ ounces carragheen moss
1¼ cups sugar
4 ounces semisweet chocolate
½ teaspoon peanut oil
⅓ cup water
1 cup strong coffee
1 tablespoon Irish whiskey
grated chocolate, to decorate
lightly whipped cream, to serve

SERVES 4

1 Pour the milk into a heavy-based saucepan. Add the carragheen moss and 2 tablespoons of sugar. Bring to a boil. Reduce the heat and simmer for 15 minutes.

2 Meanwhile, using a sharp chopping knife, chop the chocolate into small pieces or grate roughly. Remove the milk from the heat and stir in the chocolate until it has all melted.

3 Strain the chocolate mixture through a fine strainer. Very lightly grease four teacups with peanut oil, then pour in the chocolate carragheen. Chill until set.

4 Pour the water and remaining sugar into a heavy-based saucepan. Heat gently, stirring until the sugar dissolves. Remove the spoon and continue to heat the syrup until it turns a pale golden color.

5 Pour in the coffee and stir over gentle heat until smooth. Remove from the heat and cool. Stir in the whiskey. Allow to cool.

6 Turn each mousse onto a plate and pour some sauce around each one. Serve with cream and decorate with grated chocolate.

COOK'S TIP
Carragheen moss is a seaweed harvested on the west coast of Ireland. It can be eaten as a vegetable like spinach, but it is also available dried and used as a thickening agent. Look for it in health food shops.

MARMALADE PUDDING

A delicious steamed orange and ginger pudding that is very simple to make. It's tastiest if you use a good quality, tangy, thick-cut peel marmalade that's not too sweet.

INGREDIENTS
1 cup self-rising flour
pinch of salt
1 teaspoon ground ginger
1 cup shredded suet
2 cups fresh white bread crumbs
8 tablespoons dark brown sugar
8 tablespoons marmalade, plus
4 tablespoons to serve
2 tablespoons milk
light cream and orange slices, to serve

SERVES 4–6

1 Grease a 3¾ cup ovenproof bowl. Sift the flour, salt and ginger into a large bowl. Add the shredded suet, fresh bread crumbs and sugar and mix thoroughly.

2 Add the marmalade and milk, mixing thoroughly to form a wet, dough-like mixture. Pour into the prepared bowl. The mixture should fill three-quarters of the bowl. Cover with a double layer of wax paper and secure with string.

3 Steam the pudding for 2½ hours in a double boiler with a tight-fitting lid. Check the water halfway through the cooking time. Lift out the bowl and remove the paper. Run a knife around the edge of the bowl, invert onto a plate and turn out. Warm the remaining marmalade in a small pan with 2 tablespoons water and serve with the pudding with cream and orange slices.

> ### COOK'S TIP
> This pudding is best served immediately as it becomes heavy if left to stand for too long.

PRALIE APPLE PIE WITH HONEY

This deliciously sweet apple pie is made with potato pastry which cooks to a thin, crisp crust.

INGREDIENTS
8 ounces potatoes
1 cup flour
8 tablespoons sugar
½ teaspoon baking powder
pinch of salt
2 cooking apples
1 egg, beaten
2 tablespoons clear honey, to serve

SERVES 4

1 Cut the potatoes into even-size chunks. Put into a saucepan and bring to a boil, then cover and cook for 20 minutes.

2 Drain the potatoes and dry out over a high heat for 1 minute until all traces of moisture have evaporated. Mash well in a bowl. Preheat the oven to 350°F.

3 Add the flour, 4 tablespoons of the sugar, baking powder and salt and mix thoroughly to form a soft dough.

4 Place the dough on a lightly floured surface and divide it in half. Roll out one half to an 8-inch round. Transfer to a lightly greased cookie sheet.

5 Peel, core and thinly slice the apples. Arrange them on top of the pastry. Sprinkle with the remaining sugar. Brush the edges of the pastry with beaten egg.

6 Roll out the remaining pastry to a 10-inch round, then lay it over the apples. Seal the pastry edges together and brush with the remaining beaten egg.

7 Cook in the oven for 30 minutes until golden. Serve hot in slices, with a little honey drizzled over each serving.

CARROT PUDDING

A light steamed pudding made with grated carrot, plump golden raisins and a hint of orange.

INGREDIENTS
8 tablespoons self-rising flour
1 teaspoon baking powder
pinch of grated nutmeg
1 carrot
1 cup fresh white bread crumbs
8 tablespoons shredded vegetable suet
4 tablespoons golden raisins
grated rind of 1 orange
1 egg
½ cup low-fat milk
sugar and whipped cream, to serve

SERVES 4

1 Lightly grease a 3¾ cup ovenproof bowl. Sift the flour, baking powder and nutmeg into a mixing bowl.

2 Finely grate the carrot and add to the flour mixture. Stir in the bread crumbs, suet, golden raisins and orange rind.

3 Beat the egg and the milk together, then stir into the dry ingredients to form a smooth dropping consistency.

4 Spoon the mixture into the prepared ovenproof bowl. Cover the bowl with two layers of wax paper, folded in the middle to allow room for expansion, and secure with string.

5 Steam for 2 hours in a double boiler with a tight-fitting lid. Check the water halfway through the cooking time and add more, if necessary. Remove the wax paper and turn out the pudding onto a plate. Dust with a little sugar and serve with chilled whipped cream.

BROWN BREAD ICE CREAM

This uniquely flavored ice cream could be described as the poor person's praline. Chunks of brown bread are caramelized with brown sugar, then crushed into creamy ice cream.

INGREDIENTS
2 cups brown bread crumbs
4 tablespoons brown sugar
4 eggs, separated
8 tablespoons sugar
⅔ cup heavy cream
1¼ cups buttermilk
fresh raspberries, to serve (optional)

SERVES 4–6

1 Preheat the oven to 400°F. Put the bread crumbs onto a baking tray.

2 Sprinkle the brown sugar over the bread crumbs and place in the oven. Bake for 20 minutes until the sugar has caramelized over the bread. Cool on the tray.

3 Put the eggs and sugar into a heat proof bowl. Heat a little water in a pan until simmering. Place the bowl with the egg yolks and sugar over the pan.

4 Whisk the egg yolks and sugar with an electric mixer for 5 minutes until it looks like mousse and has doubled in bulk. Remove the bowl from the pan and whisk until the mixture holds a trail.

5 Whip the cream until it forms soft peaks. Fold the buttermilk into the cream, then fold into the egg yolk mixture. Break the bread up with a rolling pin and stir into the mixture.

6 Whisk the egg whites until holding soft peaks and fold into the mixture. Pour into a shallow container and freeze for 3 hours.

7 Take out of the freezer and stir with a fork to break up the ice crystals. Freeze until hard. Transfer to the fridge for 30 minutes before serving with raspberries.

BREAD PUDDING

T his moist fruit pudding is delicious served hot with vanilla ice cream or cold, cut into slices.

INGREDIENTS
8 thick slices stale white bread
1¼ cups dried fruit
¾ cup brown sugar
grated rind of 1 lemon
1 teaspoon mixed spice
3 eggs, beaten
1 tablespoon butter
light cream, to serve

SERVES 4–6

1 Preheat the oven to 350°F. Grease an 8-inch round cake pan. Put the bread into a bowl and soak in plenty of water (about 5 cups) for 30 minutes. Drain off the water and squeeze out the excess moisture from the bread.

2 Mash the bread with a fork and stir in the dried fruit, sugar, lemon rind, mixed spice and eggs, until well combined.

3 Spoon the mixture into the prepared cake pan. Dot the top of the pudding with butter, then bake for 1½ hours. Serve warm or let stand until completely cool and cut into slices. Serve with light cream. Sprinkle with a little extra brown sugar, if liked.

IRISH COFFEE

T he ultimate Irish beverage, this was invented at Shannon airport to welcome passengers in the cold winter months. I've included this in the dessert section because, as the Irish say, "there's eating and drinking in it!"

INGREDIENTS
4 teaspoons sugar
2½ cups strong hot coffee
4 measures Irish whiskey
1¼ cups thick heavy cream

MAKES 4

1 Divide the sugar among four stemmed, heat proof glasses. Put a metal teaspoon in each glass.

2 Carefully pour in the hot coffee and stir to dissolve the sugar.

3 Stir a measure of whiskey into each glass. Remove the teaspoon and hold it upside-down over the glass.

4 Slowly pour the cream over the back of the spoon on to the hot coffee so that it floats on the surface. Serve immediately.

APPLE CAKE

This cake has a thick layer of apples, raisins and hazelnuts baked between sweet sponge. It is just as delicious served cold with sweet whipped cream or yogurt, but you'll be lucky if it lasts that long.

INGREDIENTS

1 pound cooking apples
grated rind and juice of 1 lemon
¾ cup butter
1 cup sugar
3 eggs, beaten
2 cups self-rising flour
½ teaspoon baking powder
½ teaspoon ground cinnamon
5 tablespoons raisins
2 tablespoons chopped hazelnuts
4 tablespoons confectioners' sugar, to decorate

MAKES A 9-INCH CAKE

1 Preheat the oven to 350°F. Grease and base line a 9-inch round cake pan. Peel, core and thinly slice the cooking apples. Sprinkle with the lemon juice and set aside.

2 Cream the butter, lemon rind and all but 1 tablespoon of the sugar until light and fluffy. Beat in the eggs a little at a time. Sift the flour and baking powder together. Fold into the creamed mixture.

3 Spoon half of the mixture into the prepared cake pan. Arrange the apple slices on top. Mix the remaining 1 tablespoon of the sugar and the cinnamon together. Sprinkle evenly on the apples.

4 Scatter the raisins and hazelnuts on top. Smooth the remaining cake mixture over the raisins and hazelnuts. Bake for 1 hour. Cool in the pan for 15 minutes, then turn out and dust with confectioners' sugar.

CHOCOLATE POTATO CAKE

This is a very rich, moist chocolate cake, topped with a thin layer of chocolate icing. Use a good quality semisweet chocolate for best results and serve with whipped cream.

INGREDIENTS
1 cup sugar
generous 1 cup butter
4 eggs, separated
10 ounces semi-sweet chocolate
¾ cup ground almonds
1¾ cups mashed potato
2 cups self-rising flour
1 teaspoon ground cinnamon
3 tablespoons milk
whipped cream, to serve

MAKES A 9-INCH CAKE

1 Preheat the oven to 350°F. Grease and base line a 9-inch round cake pan with wax paper.

2 Cream the sugar and 1 cup of the butter together until light and fluffy. Beat in the egg yolks one at a time.

3 Finely chop or grate 6 ounces of the chocolate and stir into the cake mixture with the ground almonds. Push the mashed potato through a strainer and stir it into the creamed chocolate mixture.

4 Sift the flour and cinnamon together and fold into the mixture with the milk.

5 Whisk the egg whites until stiff, but not dry, and fold into the mixture. Spoon into the lined pan and bake for 1¼ hours. Allow the cake to cool slightly in the pan, then turn out and cool on a wire rack.

6 Meanwhile, break up the remaining chocolate into a bowl and stand it over a saucepan of hot water. Add the remaining butter in small pieces and stir well until smooth and glossy.

7 Trim the top of the cake so that it is level and smooth over the chocolate icing. Allow to set. Serve with whipped cream.

FRUIT SCONES

The recipe for scones was brought to Ireland when the English gentry first settled there in the 1800s. The Irish quickly adapted this popular tea-time cake to suit their tastes.

INGREDIENTS

2 cups flour

3 tablespoons butter

1 tablespoon sugar

1 teaspoon baking powder

4 tablespoons golden raisins

2 eggs

1½ tablespoons milk

jam and cream, to serve

MAKES 8

2 Stir in the sugar, baking powder and golden raisins and mix well together.

4 Turn out the dough onto a floured board and knead lightly. Flatten to about 1-inch thick. Stamp out circles using a plain cutter. Transfer to a cookie sheet.

1 Preheat the oven to 400°F. Sift the flour into a bowl. Rub in the butter with your fingertips.

3 Beat 1 egg. Make a well in the center of the flour mixture, then mix in the beaten egg and enough milk to form a soft dough.

5 Beat the other egg and brush on the scones. Bake for 15–20 minutes. Cool, then serve with jam and cream.

SODA BREAD

F resh homemade soda bread makes the perfect accompaniment to hearty dishes, such as Leek and Thyme Soup and Coddle.

INGREDIENTS
4 cups flour
1 teaspoon salt
1 teaspoon baking soda
1⅔ cups buttermilk

MAKES 1 LOAF

1 Preheat the oven to 450°F. Sift the flour, salt and baking soda into a bowl. Make a well in the center and pour in the buttermilk.

2 Using one hand, slowly incorporate the flour into the milk to give a soft, but not sticky, dough.

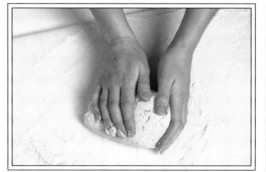

3 Turn onto a floured board and knead lightly for 1 minute until smooth. Smooth and shape into a round about 1½ inches high. Cut a deep cross from one edge to the other. Place on a floured cookie sheet.

4 Bake for 15 minutes. Reduce the heat to 400°F and bake for another 30 minutes. To test if the bread is cooked, tap the bottom of the bread which should sound hollow. Cool on a wire rack.

COOK'S TIP
For good soda bread it's important to use buttermilk, as its reaction with the baking soda helps the bread rise. If you can't buy buttermilk, use sour milk or sour your own fresh milk with a few teaspoons of lemon juice.

INDEX